SUPERSTATS
EXTREME
PLANET

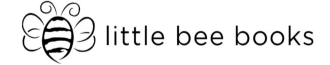

little bee books

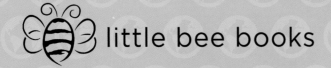

An imprint of Bonnier Publishing Group
853 Broadway, New York, New York 10003

Project managed and commissioned by Dynamo Limited
    Consultant: Mike Goldsmith
    Author: Moria Butterfield
    Editor/Picture research: Dynamo Limited
    Design: Dynamo Limited
    Index: Marie Lorimer

Manufactured in China (025)

Printed in Guang Dong, China

First Edition 2 4 6 8 10 9 7 5 3 1

ISBN 978-1-4998-0084-5

www.littlebeebooks.com

www.bonnierpublishing.com

SUPERSTATS
EXTREME
PLANET

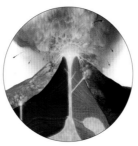

CONTENTS

🌍 FLOODS AND DROUGHT

It's always raining somewhere in the world—sometimes so heavily that floods occur. Droughts happen when rain fails to fall for long periods of time.

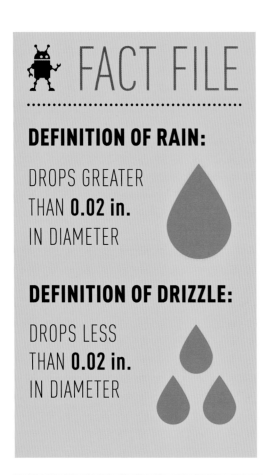

🤖 FACT FILE

DEFINITION OF RAIN:

DROPS GREATER THAN **0.02 in.** IN DIAMETER

DEFINITION OF DRIZZLE:

DROPS LESS THAN **0.02 in.** IN DIAMETER

^ HEAVY RAIN IN INDIA

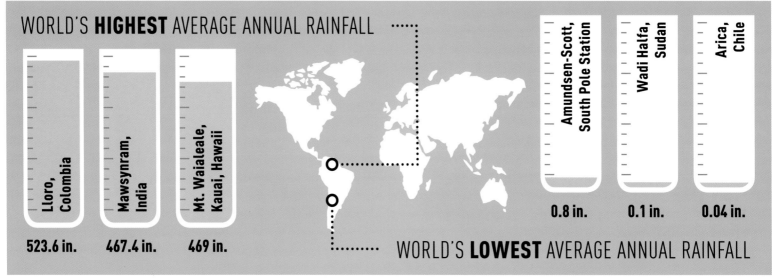

WORLD'S **HIGHEST** AVERAGE ANNUAL RAINFALL

Lloro, Colombia	Mawsynram, India	Mt. Waialeale, Kauai, Hawaii		Amundsen-Scott, South Pole Station	Wadi Halfa, Sudan	Arica, Chile
523.6 in.	467.4 in.	469 in.		0.8 in.	0.1 in.	0.04 in.

WORLD'S **LOWEST** AVERAGE ANNUAL RAINFALL

17.6
MILLION TONS

The estimated amount of raindrops falling to the surface of Earth every second. Roughly the same amount of water evaporates from the planet every second, too, from oceans, rivers, and lakes.

5
mph

The average speed of a raindrop, though this can rise up to 22 mph.

$6
BILLION

The average amount of money spent each year on damage caused by flooding in the USA.

ACID RAIN

The name given to rain made acidic by particles of pollution. Over time, acid rain can even eat away stone.

400
YEARS

No rain at all fell on the Atacama for 400 years, between the 1570s and 1970s.

The Atacama Desert in South America is the planet's most rainless place. It gets around 4 in. of rain every 1,000 years.

Some parts of the Atacama are so dry that there is no living thing, not even a tiny insect or a blade of grass.

🌍 RUNNING RIVERS

From straight and narrow to broad and winding, freshwater rivers of all shapes and sizes follow a path across the land on a journey to meet the sea.

THE LONGEST RIVER

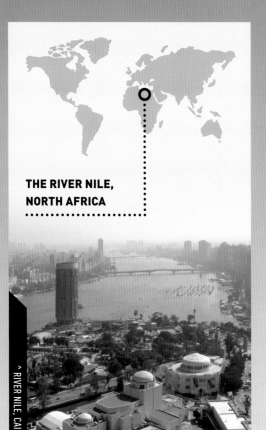

THE RIVER NILE, NORTH AFRICA

^ RIVER NILE, CAIRO

The Nile's name comes from the Ancient Greek word Neilos, *which means a valley.*

🤖 FACT FILE

⊿ The Nile is the longest river in the world, flowing for 4,132 miles.

⊿ On its journey, the Nile runs through several countries in northeast Africa.

⊿ It runs through Cairo, the capital city of Egypt.

⊿ The Nile used to flood every year between June and September until the Aswan Dam was built in the 1960s.

⊿ The Nile provides a major transport system, and traveling by boat is still a popular way to get around.

⊿ The ancient Egyptians called the Nile *Iteru*, meaning "river."

Many animals live along the Nile, including the Nile crocodile—one of the biggest crocs in the world! It can grow up to 20 ft. long.

THE PLANET'S **LONGEST** RIVERS:

1. NILE, Egypt .... **4,132 miles**
2. AMAZON, South America .... **4,000 miles**
3. YANGTZE, China .... **3,917 miles**
4. MISSISSIPPI-MISSOURI, USA
   .... **3,902 miles**
5. YENISEI, Siberia .... **3,445 miles**
6. YELLOW, China .... **3,398 miles**
7. OB-IRTYSH, Siberia .... **3,364 miles**
8. CONGO, Africa .... **2,922 miles**
9. AMUR, China and Russia.... **2,763 miles**
10. LENA, Russia .... **2,736 miles**

DEEPEST

722 FEET

That's how deep the water gets in the Congo, the deepest river in the world.

FILTHY WATERS

Many rivers are polluted, but the Citarum River in Indonesia is truly shocking! It's the filthiest river on the planet, and in some spots there's so much trash floating in it that you can't even see the water.

8 TRILLION GALLONS

The amount of water pumping out of the mouth of the Amazon river every day.

The Amazon is the world's biggest river, carrying the most water.

^ AMAZON RIVER, BRAZIL

860 *days*

...that's 2 years, 4 months, and 8 days!

The time it took Briton Ed Stafford to walk the length of the Amazon. He was the first person ever to do so.

SHORTEST

201 FEET

The length of the shortest river on the planet, the Roe River in the USA.

GOLD!

It's possible to find flakes of gold in some rivers, washed down from rocks. In 1848, gold was found in the American River in California, and it started the famous Gold Rush, when thousands turned up to search for gold!

🌐 WONDROUS WATERFALLS

When river or stream water gushes down a steep drop it's called a waterfall. Big or small, waterfalls are spectacular to see.

FACT FILE

1. As a stream or river flows over the rocky bed below it, the water gradually washes away soft rock, such as limestone and sandstone.

2. Eventually only hard rock, such as granite, is left. This forms ledges for the water to drop over.

3. The fast-falling waters smooth and flatten out the rocks at the edge of the waterfall.

4. The forceful water carves out a plunge pool below.

NIAGARA FALLS

NIAGARA FALLS STRETCHES BETWEEN THE USA AND CANADA

NIAGARA FALLS, NORTH AMERICA'S BIGGEST WATERFALL, IS 170 FT. HIGH

681,750 GALLONS OF WATER RUSH OVER THE BIGGEST SECTION, THE HORSESHOE FALLS, EVERY SECOND

WATER FROM THE HORSESHOE FALLS HITS THE BASE OF THE FALLS WITH A FORCE OF 2,509 TONS

Nick Wallenda walked across Niagara Falls on a tightrope. He battled high winds and water spray to succeed in 2012.

TOP 5 **HIGH** WATERFALLS

1. ANGEL FALLS,
   Venezuela .... **3,212 ft.**
2. TUGELA FALLS,
   South Africa .... **3,106 ft.**
3. UTIGARD FALLS,
   Norway .... **2,625 ft.**
4. MONGEFOSSEN FALLS,
   Norway .... **2,540 ft.**
5. MUTARAZI FALLS,
   Zimbabwe .... **2,499 ft.**

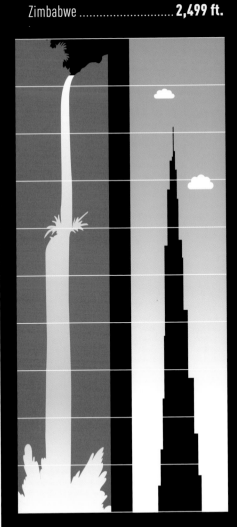

ANGEL FALLS,
Venezuela
3,200 ft.

World's tallest
building the BURJ
KHALIFA in Dubai
2,717 ft.

^ ANGEL FALLS, VENEZUELA

WAVE HELLO!

Panamanian golden
frogs live close to waterfalls.
They sometimes communicate with a
special wave, perhaps because the water
is too noisy for their croaks to be heard.

16x

The Victoria Falls in Africa is the largest
waterfall in the world, combining its
width and height. It is 354 ft. high and
just over a mile wide, the equivalent of
16 soccer fields laid end to end.

MOONBOW

During a full moon
at Victoria Falls, you
might see a moonbow.
It looks just like a
daylight rainbow, but this magic appears
through the moonlit water spray.

^ VICTORIA FALLS, AFRICA

24/7

Because of the continual
spray from the waterfall,
Victoria Falls rainforest is the
only place on the planet where
it rains all day, every day.

WIDEST TOP 5 **WIDE** WATERFALLS

1. CHUTES DE KHONE, Laos	**35,376 ft.**
2. SALTO PARA, Venezuela	**18,400 ft.**
3. CHUTES KONGOU, Gabon	**10,500 ft.**
4. CATARATAS DEL IGUAZO, Brazil/Argentina	**8,800 ft.**
5. SALTO DEL MOCONO, Argentina	**6,775 ft.**

🌐 INCREDIBLE CANYONS

A canyon is a narrow, steep-sided valley carved out of rock by a fast-moving river. Canyons (also called gorges) take millions of years to appear but provide some of the most stunning landscapes on our planet.

THE GRAND CANYON

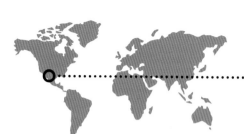

THE GRAND CANYON IN ARIZONA, USA, IS ONE OF THE BIGGEST CANYONS ON EARTH

11,000-year-old fossilized sloth bones have been found in the Grand Canyon caves.

THE CANYON WAS FORMED AS THE COLORADO RIVER GRADUALLY ERODED (WORE DOWN) THE ROCKS

NEARLY 40 STRATA (STRIPES) OF DIFFERENT ROCK HAVE BEEN EXPOSED BY THE RIVER

🤖 FACT FILE

GRAND CANYON STATS

▲ **227 MILES** *long*

▲ **1 MILE** *deep*

▲ **4 MILES** *at its narrowest point*

▲ **18 MILES** *at its widest point*

◢ It took around 6 million years for the river to carve the present Canyon shape, but some parts might even be up to 70 million years old.

◢ Native American tribes have lived around the Canyon for thousands of years, considering it a sacred place. The Paiute Tribe call it *Kaibab*, which means "mountain lying down."

THE ROCK FOUND AT THE BOTTOM IS AROUND 2 BILLION YEARS OLD

DEEPEST

3 miles

Indus Gorge in Pakistan is the world's deepest canyon. It was carved out by the powerful Indus river.

Curvy Canyon

Antelope Canyon in Arizona, USA, is famous for its cool, curvy shapes and arches. The smooth rock sculptures were created when flash floods eroded soft sandstone and left behind harder rock.

^ ANTELOPE CANYON, USA

^ INDUS GORGE, PAKISTAN

1,165 feet

The height of the Aizhai Bridge over Hunan's Dehang Canyon, China. It is the highest suspension bridge.

3 CANYON TYPES

BOX CANYON

A canyon with three sides and only one entrance in and out. It forms as sections of wall collapse farther and farther back into the land.

SLOT CANYON

A narrow corridor formed by rushing water. It may be only a few feet wide, but may drop several hundred feet to the ground.

SUBMARINE CANYON

Similar in appearance to a land canyon, but this type is carved out by ocean currents and is found on the sea floor (see pg. 19).

18,871 FEET LONG

The length of the world's longest cable car. It travels across the Vorotan River Gorge in Armenia.

THE BIG ONE

The Yarlung Tsangpo Grand Canyon in the Himalayas is the world's longest and deepest canyon.

▲ 17,567 FEET deep
▲ 308 MILES long

? *Six rattlesnake species live in the Grand Canyon, including the Grand Canyon pink rattlesnake. It's super-hard to see against the pink rocks!*

EXTREME LAKES

A lake is a large pool of water with a river or stream feeding into it or running out of it. It's possible to have a lake of red-hot lava, too.

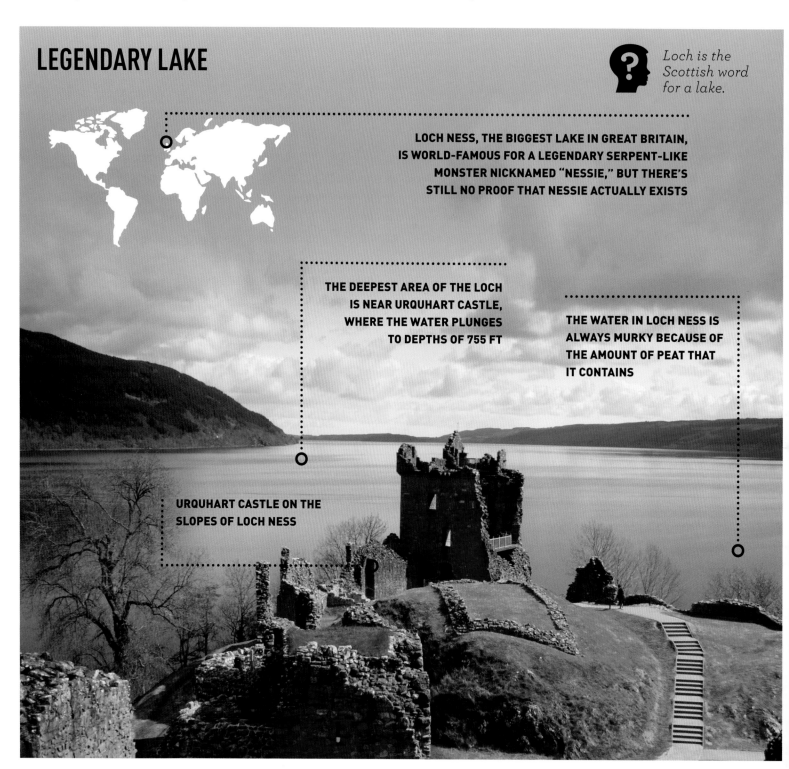

LEGENDARY LAKE

? *Loch is the Scottish word for a lake.*

LOCH NESS, THE BIGGEST LAKE IN GREAT BRITAIN, IS WORLD-FAMOUS FOR A LEGENDARY SERPENT-LIKE MONSTER NICKNAMED "NESSIE," BUT THERE'S STILL NO PROOF THAT NESSIE ACTUALLY EXISTS

THE DEEPEST AREA OF THE LOCH IS NEAR URQUHART CASTLE, WHERE THE WATER PLUNGES TO DEPTHS OF 755 FT

THE WATER IN LOCH NESS IS ALWAYS MURKY BECAUSE OF THE AMOUNT OF PEAT THAT IT CONTAINS

URQUHART CASTLE ON THE SLOPES OF LOCH NESS

DEEPEST

1,300 FEET
BELOW SEA LEVEL

The lowest lake on the planet, the Dead Sea, between Israel and Jordan.

The Dead Sea is one of the saltiest lakes in the world. The salty water is more dense than fresh water, so swimmers can easily float on their backs while reading a book!

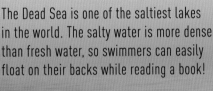

TOXIC
SHOCK!

Lake Karachay in Russia is possibly the most polluted place on Earth. It was used as a nuclear waste site, and its radiation levels are so deadly that just one hour of exposure would be enough to kill someone.

DEVIL'S *BATH*

Sulfur in the water gives the Devil's Bath lake in New Zealand its glowing green appearance, not to mention its smell of rotten eggs!

 = **20%**

The Great Lakes of North America include five lakes—**Michigan, Huron, Erie, Ontario**, and **Superior**. Together, they contain over 20% of the world's freshwater supply.

^ LAGUNA SALADA DE TORREVIEJA, SPAIN

^ DEVIL'S BATH LAKE, NEW ZEALAND

Treasures were thrown into lakes in ancient times. Lake Titicaca on the border of Peru and Bolivia is said to hide priceless golden treasures thrown in by Inca priests.

In the Pink

Sometimes saltwater lakes turn pink and look as if they've been filled with strawberry milkshakes. The color change is caused by a special algae which grows in high levels of salt.

282 MILLION
CUBIC FEET

The amount of molten rock in the world's largest lava lake on Mount Nyiragongo in the Congo, Africa. Don't try swimming here!

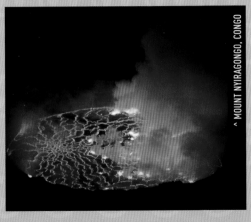

^ MOUNT NYIRAGONGO, CONGO

187,000+

That's how many lakes exist in Finland, and it's how it got its nickname "Land of the Thousand Lakes."

🌍 MONSTER WAVES

Mega freak waves can hit suddenly and without warning, even when the sea appears calm.

WHY BIG WAVES?

STORM WAVES AT THE DOURO RIVER HARBOR, PORTUGAL

🤖 FACT FILE

◤ A storm surge is a change in sea level caused by a storm. It can cause crashing waves and widespread flooding in coastal areas.

◤ Freak waves can occur far out at sea when strong winds and sea currents cause single waves to merge, forming one giant monster wave.

◤ Tsunami waves are caused by an earthquake, volcanic eruption, or landslide displacing lots of water.

TSUNAMI FACTS

◢ If a large amount of water is displaced suddenly (by an earthquake, for instance), it leads to a series of tsunami waves called a "wave train."

◢ The gap between each wave in a wave train is called the "wave period." It can be a few minutes or up to two hours.

◢ Later waves, such as the fifth or sixth, are usually much bigger and stronger than the first.

◢ Tsunami waves travel at super-fast speeds over the sea. Then the tsunami waves slow suddenly and rise up higher before crashing down on the coastline.

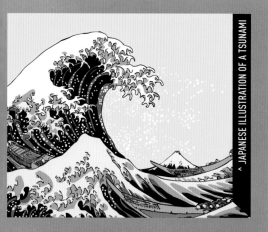

< JAPANESE ILLUSTRATION OF A TSUNAMI

OCEAN *TRAGEDY*

The 2004 Indian Ocean tsunami was one of the deadliest natural disasters in human history. At least 290,000 people were killed or left missing. It was caused by an undersea earthquake.

Some animals, such as elephants, seem to sense tsunamis coming. They tend to head for higher ground before disaster strikes.

FASTEST

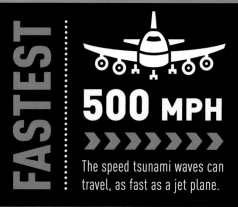

500 MPH

The speed tsunami waves can travel, as fast as a jet plane.

The Pacific Tsunami Warning System in Hawaii measures earthquakes and water levels to try to predict tsunamis.

80%

The percentage of tsunamis that occur in the Pacific "Ring of Fire" (see pg. 25) because there is so much earthquake and volcano activity there.

DEADLY KATRINA

In 2005, Hurricane Katrina brought a storm surge of more than 26 ft. to US coastal areas. It caused severe flooding, including most of New Orleans.

1720 *FEET HIGH*

The height of the tallest wave ever recorded (5.6 times higher than the Statue of Liberty). It reached Lituya Bay in Alaska in 1958.

60 MPH

Speed at which waves generated by wind may travel.

ATLANTIS

The myth of Atlantis, a mysterious, lost underwater city, may well have begun when a tsunami hit the island of Crete around 3,500 years ago, overwhelming the Minoans who lived there.

100 *FEET HIGH*

The height of the wave ridden by Brazilian surfer Carlos Burle off the coast of Portugal in 2013.

DEEPEST SEA

It takes hours for submersibles to reach the deepest regions of the world's oceans, and the extreme water pressure makes manned sub visits to the freezing gloom very risky.

SUPERSTRONG SIDES

In the deepest spots, water pressure can be up to a thousand times the atmospheric pressure we feel at sea level on Earth's surface. Deep-diving subs must be built with extra-strong titanium walls and reinforced windows.

FRENCH RESEARCH SUB *NAUTILE* CAN EXPLORE WRECKS, MAKE VIDEOS, AND COLLECT SAMPLES FROM THE DEEP SEABED

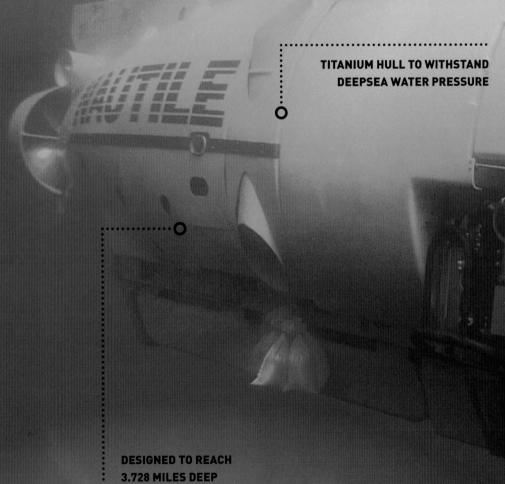

TITANIUM HULL TO WITHSTAND DEEPSEA WATER PRESSURE

DESIGNED TO REACH 3.728 MILES DEEP

FACT FILE

DEEPEST OCEAN SPOTS

Across the world there is a network of deep underwater trenches:

1. PACIFIC OCEAN
Mariana Trench = 6.9 miles

2. ATLANTIC OCEAN
Puerto Rico Trench = 5.4 miles

3. INDIAN OCEAN
Java Trench = 4.8 miles

4. SOUTHERN OCEAN
South Sandwich Trench = 4.5 miles

5. ARCTIC OCEAN
Eurasian Basin = 3.4 miles

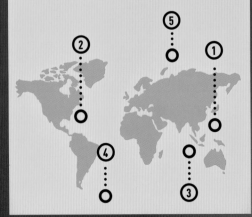

 Deep down, the seabed looks like a rocky desert covered in muddy ooze formed from the remains of dead creatures and plant plankton.

ROOM FOR THREE CREW, WITH OXYGEN SUPPLY FOR UP TO 8 HOURS

MARIANA TRENCH

◢ A trench 1,580 miles long and 43 miles wide, it is the world's deepest point, located in the western Pacific Ocean.

◢ If the world's tallest mountain, Mount Everest, were put into the Mariana Trench, there would still be 1.4 miles of water above it.

◢ The deepest part is named Challenger Deep. As of 2012, only three people had reached this spot.

◢ In 2012, Deepsea Challenger made the first solo dive to the bottom of the Mariana Trench.

◢ It took two hours and 36 minutes for Deepsea Challenger to reach the bottom.

DEEPSEA CHALLENGER

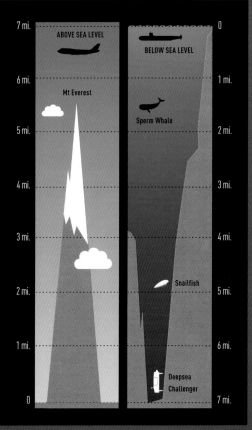

ABOVE SEA LEVEL

Mt Everest

BELOW SEA LEVEL

Sperm Whale

Snailfish

Deepsea Challenger

7 mi. · 6 mi. · 5 mi. · 4 mi. · 3 mi. · 2 mi. · 1 mi. · 0

0 · 1 mi. · 2 mi. · 3 mi. · 4 mi. · 5 mi. · 6 mi. · 7 mi.

At home *in the deep!*

An unknown shrimplike species (right) was filmed eating bait put out by a Chinese sub exploring 4.35 miles down in the Mariana Trench. The deepest ever recorded fish was a snailfish, at 5.06 miles.

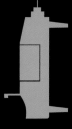

> MARIANA TRENCH, PACIFIC OCEAN

ROBOT ARM FOR TAKING SAMPLES

50x ⬇

The water pressure at the bottom of the mariana Trench is equivalent to the weight of piling 50 jumbo jets on top of a person.

? *Sunlight from the ocean surface penetrates to about 3,280 ft. deep. Below that depth, submersibles can only see using their own lights.*

🌍 WATERY TRAPS

When water currents traveling in opposite directions meet, they can create mesmerizing swirling whirlpools. Most are pretty gentle, but some turn into powerful, dangerous vortexes.

 Powerful whirlpools have been known to suck swimmers to their deaths, but there's no proof that they've ever swallowed a large ship.

NARUTO WHIRLPOOLS

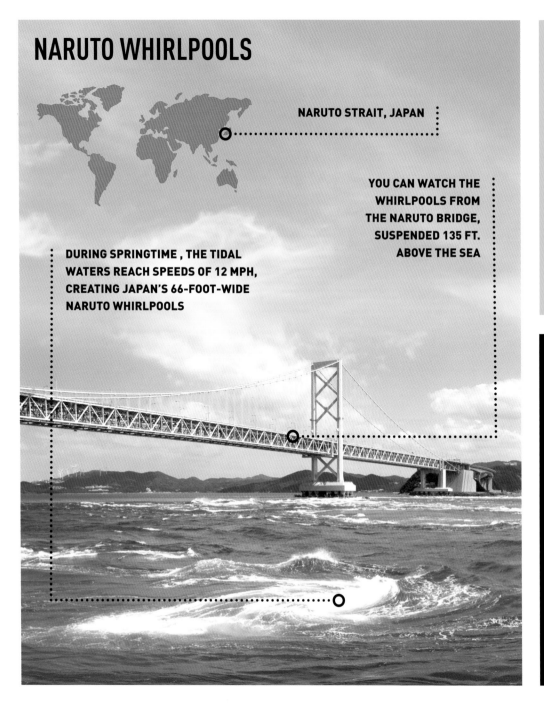

NARUTO STRAIT, JAPAN

YOU CAN WATCH THE WHIRLPOOLS FROM THE NARUTO BRIDGE, SUSPENDED 135 FT. ABOVE THE SEA

DURING SPRINGTIME , THE TIDAL WATERS REACH SPEEDS OF 12 MPH, CREATING JAPAN'S 66-FOOT-WIDE NARUTO WHIRLPOOLS

 FACT FILE

WHIRLPOOL WORDS

◣ **MAELSTROM**—the name for a powerful whirlpool.

◣ **VORTEX**—a whirlpool with a strong downward-sucking current.

◣ **STRAIT**—a narrow channel of water connecting two seas or two larger bodies of water, home to the most powerful whirlpools.

TOP 5 **FASTEST** WHIRLPOOLS

1. SALTSTRAUMEN,
   Norway .... **23 mph**

2. MOSKSTRAUMEN,
   Norway .... **17.3 mph**

3. OLD SOW,
   USA-Canada .... **17.1 mph**

4. NARUTO WHIRLPOOLS,
   Japan .... **12 mph**

5. CORRYVRECKAN,
   Scotland .... **11 mph**

0.25 MILES WIDE

The size of a whirlpool created suddenly when drilling equipment accidentally broke into a salt mine under US Lake Peigneur in 1980. Three and a half billion gallons of water eventually disappeared down the hole, along with drilling equipment, boats, trees, and earth.

Old Sow is a whirlpool off the coast of New Brunswick, Canada. It is thought to be named after the piglike grunts that its churning waters make.

In ancient Greek mythology, a sea monster called Charybdis would swallow water and then burp it all out again to create whirlpools that trapped ships.

1 BILLION TONS

Photos from space have helped to reveal massive, slow-moving whirlpools in the southern Atlantic Ocean, bigger than the size of a city and containing up to a billion tons of water.

TSUNAMI SWIRL

In 2011, Japan's Tohoku earthquake created a giant whirlpool in the Pacific Ocean near the coastal town of Oarai.

^ SALTSTRAUMEN, NORWAY

3,000 YEARS

That's how long Saltstraumen, the world's fastest whirlpool, has been spinning. It's 33 ft. wide and 16 ft. deep.

AMAZING SEA SPOTS

Sea caves and ocean sinkholes are among the most beautiful locations on Earth.

 FACT FILE

GREAT BLUE HOLE STATS

◢ **984 FEET WIDE**

◢ **407 FEET DEEP**

◢ Stalactites from the flooded sinkhole date its beginnings to 15,000 years ago.

◢ It's one of the finest diving sites in the world. Fish living here include parrotfish and reef sharks.

THE GREAT BLUE HOLE, BELIZE

THE GREAT BLUE HOLE, BELIZE

Sea caves are carved by powerful, crashing waves that batter cliffs and erode (wear down) their rocks.

THE GREAT BLUE HOLE IS A SUBMARINE SINKHOLE— A GIANT PLUNGING CAVE WITH VERTICAL WALLS, FILLED WITH SEAWATER—SITUATED ON A CORAL REEF OFF THE COAST OF BELIZE

ITS WATERS APPEAR TO CHANGE COLOR, FROM TURQUOISE TO DEEP BLUE, DEPENDING ON HOW NEAR OR FAR AWAY YOU ARE

 Ocean sinkholes were formed thousands of years ago and then filled up with seawater as sea levels rose over time.

TOP ROCKS

Benagil sea cave in Portugal is regarded as one of the most beautiful caves on Earth. It has its own cave beach!

^ BENAGIL, PORTUGAL

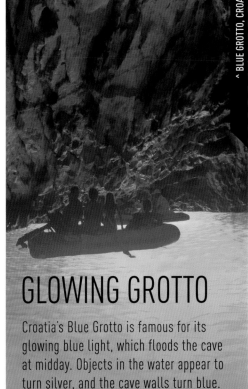

^ BLUE GROTTO, CROATIA

DEEPEST

663 FEET

The depth of the world's deepest sea hole, Dean's Blue Hole in the Bahamas. Divers can reach it through an underwater entrance.

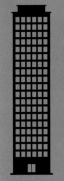

50-STORIES

World champion freediver Guillaume Nery traveled to the bottom of Dean's Blue Hole—farther than the height of a 50-story skyscraper—then back again without breathing!

GLOWING GROTTO

Croatia's Blue Grotto is famous for its glowing blue light, which floods the cave at midday. Objects in the water appear to turn silver, and the cave walls turn blue.

SINGING CAVE

This Scottish sea cave is famous for the strange echoing sounds it makes as waves lap against its walls. Its nickname is the Cave of Melody.

^ FINGAL'S CAVE, SCOTLAND

The waters inside the Italian Blue Grotto sea cave on Capri are illuminated by sunlight shining through openings beneath. If you put your hand in the water it will appear to glow, and people once used to stay away because they thought the glowing was witch's magic!

Blowholes are fountains of seawater that shoot up through holes in the coastal rock. They can soar up hundreds of feet high.

125 FEET HIGH

The height of the main cavern in America's largest sea cave system, Sea Lion Caves in Oregon, USA. The cavern is longer and wider than a football field and home to noisy sea lions. You might be able to spot them from home, on the cave's webcam.

SHAKING WORLD

Earth's surface is made up of large pieces called tectonic plates, like the pieces of a jigsaw puzzle. They slowly move around and sometimes collide, causing the ground to shudder. We call this scary shaking an earthquake.

 Earthquake tremors can trigger other natural disasters, including tsunamis (giant waves), landslides, and avalanches.

EARTHQUAKE EFFECT

ERCIŞ, VAN, TURKEY

IN OCTOBER 2011, A POWERFUL QUAKE HIT ERCIŞ IN TURKEY, MEASURING 7.2 ON THE RICHTER SCALE

HUNDREDS LOST THEIR LIVES AND THOUSANDS OF BUILDINGS WERE DAMAGED

FACT FILE

1. Tectonic plates don't always glide smoothly past each other. Sometimes they get jammed and pressure builds up under Earth's crust.

2. Where two plates meet is called a plate boundary. The rocks here may be pushed along or up by the pressure.

3. The rock movement creates waves of energy called shockwaves that shake the surface. The spot where the rocks move is called the focus.

4. The point on the Earth's surface where the shockwaves hit is called the epicenter.

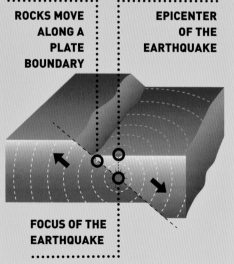

ROCKS MOVE ALONG A PLATE BOUNDARY

EPICENTER OF THE EARTHQUAKE

FOCUS OF THE EARTHQUAKE

OFF THE **SCALE**

THE RICHTER SCALE has ten numbers used to measure the size and strength of an earthquake. You probably wouldn't feel a magnitude 1 earthquake, but anything over a magnitude of 6 would probably cause some serious damage.

0-1 ... Micro-earthquakes not felt
2 .... Indoor objects shake
3 .... Objects fall off shelves
4 .... Noticeable damage
5 .... Violent shaking
6 .... Major building damage
7 .... Can be detected all over world
8 .... Death and major destruction
9 .... Total devastation

SEISMOMETER

A machine that detects the vibrations caused by an earthquake.

THE MERCALLI SCALE has 12 numbers (in Roman numerals) measuring the effect of an earthquake on objects and buildings. Examples:

II .... Lamps swing, Windows shake.
V .... Dishes smash.
VII ...... Walls collapse.
XII ..... Total damage.

9.5

The magnitude of the largest, most powerful earthquake ever recorded. It happened in Chile on May 22, 1960.

^ CHRISTCHURCH, NEW ZEALAND

^ PACIFIC RING OF FIRE

1,300,000

The average number of earthquakes per year with magnitudes of 2.9 or less on the Richter Scale.

1 The number of earthquakes each year with a magnitude of 8.0 or more.

90%

Percentage of the planet's earthquakes that occur in the area of the Pacific Ocean called the "Ring of Fire."

1 MINUTE

The average time most earthquakes last.

Aftershocks can still occur many years after a major earthquake.

EMERGENCY LESSON

In earthquake-prone areas, school children regularly practice how to react if an earthquake hits. They crawl under their desks headfirst and crouch there until danger passes.

🌍 FIERY MOUNTAINS

A volcano is no ordinary mountain. Deep below it, super-hot liquid rock, called magma, bubbles away under Earth's surface. If pressure builds, magma is forced up to the top of the volcano where it spews out as hot lava and ash.

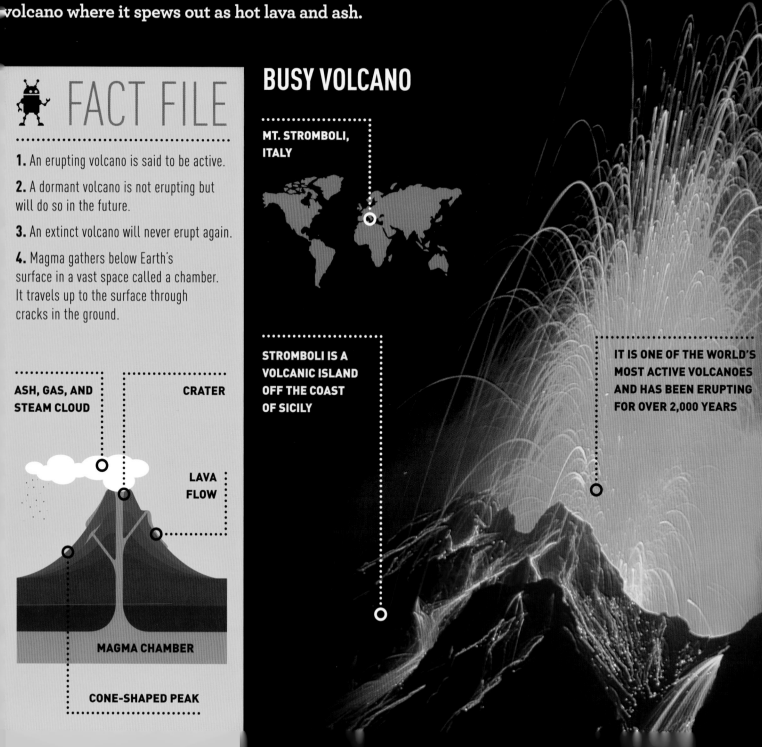

🐞 FACT FILE

1. An erupting volcano is said to be active.

2. A dormant volcano is not erupting but will do so in the future.

3. An extinct volcano will never erupt again.

4. Magma gathers below Earth's surface in a vast space called a chamber. It travels up to the surface through cracks in the ground.

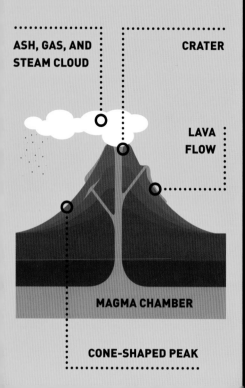

ASH, GAS, AND STEAM CLOUD

CRATER

LAVA FLOW

MAGMA CHAMBER

CONE-SHAPED PEAK

BUSY VOLCANO

MT. STROMBOLI, ITALY

STROMBOLI IS A VOLCANIC ISLAND OFF THE COAST OF SICILY

IT IS ONE OF THE WORLD'S MOST ACTIVE VOLCANOES AND HAS BEEN ERUPTING FOR OVER 2,000 YEARS

TYPES OF **VOLCANO**

A volcano's shape depends on the type of eruption that created it and the kind of material that came out.

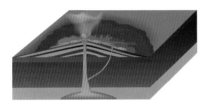

1. SHIELD VOLCANOES are shaped like upturned saucers, with gentle slopes.

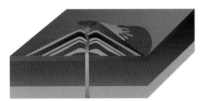

2. LAVA DOMES build up in a mound shape when lava erupts slowly out of the ground.

3. STRATA VOLCANOES are cone-shaped mountains.

1,500

The number of active volcanoes in the world.

Diamonds come from volcanoes, brought up from deep inside the earth by volcanic eruptions.

Ground-up pumice (rock) from volcano eruptions is used in some toothpastes. It's also used in makeup and bath cleaners.

119,000
SQUARE MILES

The size of Tamu Massif, the biggest volcano ever found on Earth. Its area is as large as New Mexico or the whole of the United Kingdom. It lies deep beneath the Pacific Ocean and is luckily extinct!

20–30

The number of volcanoes that erupt each year, mostly under the sea.

DUCK!

Flying hot lava chunks are called volcanic bombs. In 1935, Mount Asama in Japan fired flying 18-foot-wide volcanic bombs as far as 1,968 feet away.

1,742°F

The staggeringly high temperature that molten lava can reach.

As if the heat weren't bad enough, gas from an erupting volcano often stinks of rotten eggs!

HOT
MUD TUB!

Colombian tourists queue up to bathe in Totumo's warm, mud-filled volcano crater. The mud is said to be good for the skin.

^ TOTUMO

🌍 BUBBLING UP

Hot springs and geysers are found mainly in volcanic regions in the USA. They are spectacular to watch but can be steamy and scorching, heated by hot rocks beneath Earth.

OLD FAITHFUL GEYSER

More than half of the world's geysers can be found at Yellowstone National Park, USA, home to the largest geyser field (stretch of geysers) on Earth.

OLD FAITHFUL, THE WORLD'S MOST FAMOUS GEYSER, IN YELLOWSTONE PARK, USA

OLD FAITHFUL'S ERUPTIONS ARE 90–180 FT. HIGH

IT SHOOTS UP THOUSANDS OF GALLONS OF BOILING WATER

THE GEYSER ERUPTS EVERY 35 TO 120 MINUTES AND LASTS FROM 1½ TO 5 MINUTES

 FACT FILE

1. Water soaks into the ground and is warmed by hot volcanic rock.

2. As the water heats up it collects in an underground pool.

3. Once boiling, the highly pressurized water forces its way back to the surface through cracks and spaces, shooting up into the air as water and steam.

4. Heated groundwater begins seeping back into the underground pool, and the whole cycle begins again.

RAINBOW RING

Grand Prismatic Spring in Yellowstone National Park is the biggest hot spring in the USA and the third largest in the world. It's encircled by a stunning rainbow of colors caused by bacteria, which thrive in the mineral-rich waters.

^ GRAND PRISMATIC SPRING

1,600 FEET TALL

Waimangu Geyser in New Zealand was the highest geyser ever recorded. That's higher than the Willis Tower in Chicago!

^ FRYING PAN LAKE

BIGGEST 660 FEET

The width of Frying Pan Lake in New Zealand. Formed by a volcanic eruption in 1886, its crater is now home to the largest hot spring on Earth.

OFF THE PLANET

Geyser-like eruptions of water vapor have been spotted on the surface of Saturn's moon Enceladus, and eruptions of nitrogen have been recorded on Neptune's moon Triton.

^ NEPTUNE'S MOON TRITON

MONKEY BUSINESS

Japanese macaques are famous for bathing in hot springs near Nagano, Japan, to keep warm in the icy winter.

^ HOT SPRINGS, ICELAND

OLD SMOKY

Iceland is home to many bubbling hot springs and geysers, including Strokkur, which erupts every 5–8 minutes. The capital, Reykjavík, means "smoky bay." It was named after the steamy local waters.

1,000,000 GALLONS

The amount of hot water in Glenwood Springs, Colorado, USA, the largest hot spring swimming pool in the world. The mineral-rich water is said to be great for the skin.

🌍 TREASURE!

Our planet is awash with wondrous treasures such as precious metals and valuable stones. The tricky bit is finding them and digging them out of the ground!

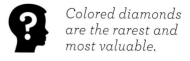 *Colored diamonds are the rarest and most valuable.*

DIAMOND HOLE

MIRNY, EASTERN SIBERIA, RUSSIA

THE MIRNY DIAMOND MINE IS 1,722 FT. DEEP AND HAS A DIAMETER OF 3,900 FT

 FACT FILE

PRECIOUS FACTS

◤ The beach at Red Ruby Bay in Scotland is well known for its tiny red rubies, but you have to look hard to spot them.

◤ You can dig for jewels at different spots around the USA. Sapphires are found at Gem Mountain in Montana and diamonds at the Crater of Diamonds State Park in Arkansas. Rubies and emeralds await in North Carolina.

◤ Go to Queensland, Australia, for some "fossicking" (prospecting) for sapphires.

◤ The finest rubies are said to come from Myanmar (Burma) and the best emeralds from Colombia, South America.

US$ **30.6** million

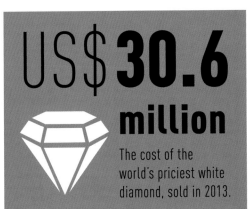

The cost of the world's priciest white diamond, sold in 2013.

MORE THAN 50% OF THE WORLD'S DIAMOND MINES ARE LOCATED IN RUSSIA

TOP 5 RAREST GEMSTONES

(values in **US$ PER CARAT**)

1. JADEITE ....**3 million**
2. RED DIAMOND ....**2–2.5 million**
3. SERENDIBITE ......**1.8–2 million**
4. BLUE GARNET ....**1.5 million**
5. PAINITE...................**50–60,000**

CARAT = A unit of weight, equal to 0.007 oz., used for gemstones.

TOP 5 *GOLD-MINING* COUNTRIES

1. **CHINA**
2. **AUSTRALIA**
3. **USA**
4. **RUSSIA**
5. **SOUTH AFRICA**

DEEPEST **2.5** MILES

The depth of the deepest mine on Earth, the Mponeng gold mine in South Africa.

When diamond fever broke out in the Namib Desert, Africa, in 1908, the town of Kolmanskop sprang up (below). It boasted plush housing, a school, hospital, and even a casino, but was abandoned in the 1950s when diamond prices fell.

FAMOUS *JEWELS*

KOH-I-NOOR DIAMOND, 106 carats, owned by the British royal family.

THE MILLENNIUM SAPPHIRE, carved with the images of 134 famous people through history. It is the size of a football.

DOM PEDRO, the world's largest aquamarine, cut into an obelisk shape.

CHINATAMANI, the world's largest luminous pearl, which glows green in the dark and weighs 6 tons. It is made of a mineral called fluorite.

THE GRAFF PINK, the world's most expensive pink diamond.

TOP 10 PRECIOUS METALS

1. **RHODIUM**
2. **PLATINUM**
3. **GOLD**
4. **RUTHENIUM**
5. **IRIDIUM**
6. **OSMIUM**
7. **PALLADIUM**
8. **RHENIUM**
9. **SILVER**
10. **INDIUM**

🌎 WETLAND WORLDS

Wetlands are areas of land that are soaked in water. The water is very shallow so trees and plants can easily grow. Wetlands are usually near streams and rivers that flood through the land.

WETLAND WORLDS

 FACT FILE

◢ During the rainy season (December to March), 80 percent of the vast Pantanal wetlands in Brazil are flooded.

◢ The Pantanal covers more than 57,915 sq. miles, making it bigger than many countries!

◢ A huge variety of plants and wildlife inhabit the Pantanal, including hundreds of bird species.

◢ Among the rarest animals found on the wetlands are giant river otters, jaguars, and hyacinth macaws.

RARE AND FEARSOME JAGUARS LIVE IN THE PANTANAL REGION.

THE PANTANAL, BRAZIL

? *Travelers must beware of quicksand on the Pantanal. Quicksand is sand so wet that it sucks down anything that stands on it.*

WETLAND *WORDS*

BOG—soft, wet, muddy ground.

MARSH—soft, wet, grassy land.

PEAT—vegetation that has rotted down over many centuries.

SWAMP—a wetland area that is forested, usually found alongside a river.

MANGROVE SWAMP—a wetland on the coast, washed by the tides, where mangrove trees grow (below).

MAD *IN MUD!*

At the World Bog Snorkeling Championships, held annually in Wales, UK, competitors swim two lengths of a 164 ft., mud-filled trench cut out of a peat bog.

^ OKEFENOKEE SWAMP, USA

^ SUDD SWAMP, SOUTH SUDAN

BIGGEST BOGS

386,102 sq. miles

The world's biggest frozen peat bog, in Western Siberia. It is as big as France and Germany put together, and scientists believe it may be slowly thawing.

20,463m sq. miles

Russia's Vasyugan Swamp, which has over 800 lakes.

3,861 sq. miles

The Sundarbands, the largest tidal mangrove swamp on the planet, found in India and Bangladesh.

1,000 sq. miles

The Okefenokee (top), the biggest swamp in the USA, on the Georgia-Florida border.

Yellow anaconda snakes, growing up to 9.8 ft. long, lurk in the waters in the Pantanal, waiting to squeeze prey to death.

FLOATING *ISLANDS*

Huge plant clumps up to 19 miles long float around on the Sudd Swamp in South Sudan. It's an almost impenetrable place, but the Nuer People live here, building their huts on patches of dry land.

10 million

The number of caiman (a type of crocodile) thought to live in the Pantanal.

DON'T *PANIC!*

Quicksand occurs on riverbanks, beaches, lakes, marshes, and close to underground springs. It's rare to be submerged by quicksand, but people tend to panic, sink deeper and become trapped.

🌐 SINKHOLES

When land disappears suddenly and unexpectedly it leaves a gaping hole in the ground known as a sinkhole. Sometimes sinkholes fill up with water to become deep, round-shaped pools.

Sinkholes have been known to swallow roads, cars, and even entire houses!

HAMILTON POOL SINKHOLE

THIS SINKHOLE WAS CREATED WHEN THE ROOF OF AN UNDERGROUND RIVER COLLAPSED

 FACT FILE

1. Acidic rainwater seeps into the soil and erodes (slowly dissolves) underground limestone rock.

2. Underground caves gradually form.

These are usually full of water, which helps to support the cave roof.

3. During a drought, the water level drops. When it rains again, the saturated ground above may become too heavy for the thin layer of rock below to support.

4. The weakened cave roof collapses without warning, forming a sinkhole.

HAMILTON POOL SINKHOLE, TEXAS, USA

HISTORY **HOLE**

Nowadays, Ik-Kil Cenote sinkhole, Mexico, is a popular bathing spot for tourists, but to the Mayans it was a sacred site. They made a sacrificial offering to the rain god by throwing young people into the pool and leaving them to drown.

^ IK-KIL CENOTE SINKHOLE, MEXICO

^ BIMMAH SINKHOLE, OMAN

Sinkhole Spa

The bright turquoise waters of Bimmah sinkhole in Oman make a fabulous outdoor swimming pool. Bathers can even enjoy a pedicure from the tiny fish that nibble their feet!

HOLEY **CITY**

The city of Berezniki in Russia is riddled with large, gaping sinkholes. This is because it's built over an old mine and the excavated land beneath is gradually eroding and collapsing.

QATTARA DEPRESSION

HOLEY WORDS!

KARST —The name given to an area where there are lots of sinkholes.

CENOTE —A water-filled sinkhole connected to underground caves and streams.

In 1994, a particularly destructive sinkhole in Florida was nicknamed "Journey to the Center of the Earth." A cavity appeared under a pile of toxic waste and poisoned 90 percent of the state's drinking water.

7,500 SQUARE MILES

The size of the Qattara Depression sinkhole in Egypt—the largest on Earth. It is roughly the shape of a giant footprint and covered with sand dunes and salt flats.

🌐 UP TOP

People are drawn to towering, snow-capped mountains. It's not just because they are awesome to look at, but also because they're great for hiking, climbing, and skiing, too.

MOUNT EVEREST

MOUNT EVEREST, HIMALAYAS, NEPAL

MOUNT EVEREST IS THE TALLEST PEAK ON EARTH, AT 29,035 FT. HIGH

TOUGH
AT THE TOP

Plenty of trees and vegetation grow at the bottom of a mountain, but farther up only ground plants thrive in the cold. Nothing grows at the peak due to harsh cold, winds, and blizzards.

AIR PRESSURE DROPS THE HIGHER UP YOU GO—IT WOULD TAKE 18.5 MINUTES TO BOIL AN EGG AT 28,000 FT.!

FACT FILE

1. Earth's crust is made up of large slabs called plates that are always moving (see pg. 24). When two collide they force earth upward, forming a mountain.

2. It takes many millions of years for mountains to form. Everest is still forming, growing around 0.156 in. every year.

3. Mountain heights are measured from sea level.

PLATES MEET

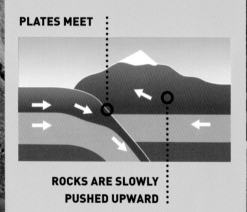

ROCKS ARE SLOWLY PUSHED UPWARD

Above 26,000 ft., the Everest air contains too little oxygen for human survival. Mountaineers have to use oxygen tanks to help them breathe.

NAMES FOR **MT. EVEREST**

CHOMOLUNGMA *(TIBETAN)* — the Tibetan mother goddess of the universe.

SAGAMARTHA *(NEPALESE)* — meaning "head of the sky."

EVEREST *(ENGLISH)* — after the 19th century British surveyor George Everest.

12,507 FEET

The height of the world's highest navigable lake, Titicaca, up in the Andes Mountains on the border of Bolivia and Peru.

In 1986, Canadian Pat Morrow became the first person to accomplish the 7-Summit Challenge by climbing the highest mountain on each world continent.

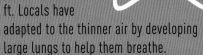

7 SUMMIT CHALLENGE

1. MOUNT EVEREST
   Asia.................................. **29,035 ft.**

2. ACONCAGUA
   South America.................. **22,831 ft.**

3. MOUNT MCKINLEY (DENALI)
   North America.................. **20,322 ft.**

4. KILIMANJARO
   Africa .... **19,341 ft.**

5. ELBRUS
   Europe............................. **18,510 ft.**

6. MOUNT VINSON
   Antarctic.......................... **16,066 ft.**

7. CARSTENZ PYRAMID
   Australasia .... **16,024 ft.**

-60°F

Winter temperatures on Mt. McKinley (also called Denali), the highest mountain in North America.

The mining town of La Rinconada, in the Peruvian Andes, is the world's highest inhabited place at 18,000 ft. Locals have adapted to the thinner air by developing large lungs to help them breathe.

About 5% of Earth's land is covered by mountain ranges.

33,464 FEET

The height of Mauna Kea in Hawaii. It is actually the world's highest mountain, but it is partly underwater below sea level.

^ MOUNT RUSHMORE

14 YEARS

The time it took to create Mount Rushmore's presidents' sculpture in South Dakota, USA. George Washington's face in the forefront is 60 ft. long.

🌍 CRAZY CLIFFS

Sheer cliffsides create stunning scenery but are constantly changing due to erosion by wind and sea.

Legend has it that the mountains here, the Troll Peaks, are the remains of two troll armies who fought a battle one night but were turned to stone at sunrise.

TROLL WALL

TROLL WALL, NORWAY

TROLL WALL IS EUROPE'S TALLEST VERTICAL CLIFF FACE, RISING 3,600 FT. ABOVE SEA LEVEL

THE CLIFF'S RIM IS LINED WITH ROCK SPIRES AND PINNACLES

IT ATTRACTS CLIMBERS BUT IT IS DANGEROUS BECAUSE THERE ARE FREQUENT ROCKFALLS, CAUSED BY EROSION

🤖 FACT FILE

1. The sea may attack the base of a cliff, wearing a notch into it.

2. The notch grows bigger, causing the overhanging part of the cliff to break off.

OVERHANG   **RETREATING CLIFF**

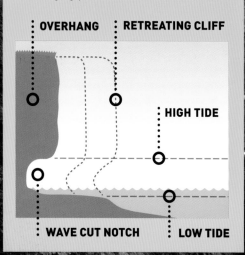

HIGH TIDE

WAVE CUT NOTCH   **LOW TIDE**

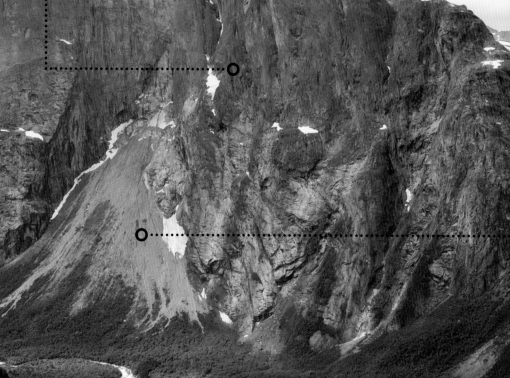

^ BASE JUMPERS

CRAZY
ON A CLIFF!

The extreme sport of base jumping involves parachuting off a fixed structure such as a high cliff.

4,101
FEET TALL

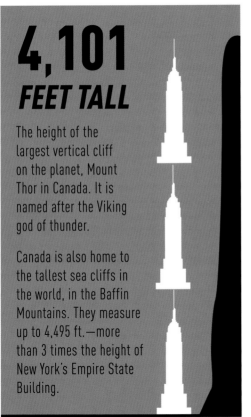

The height of the largest vertical cliff on the planet, Mount Thor in Canada. It is named after the Viking god of thunder.

Canada is also home to the tallest sea cliffs in the world, in the Baffin Mountains. They measure up to 4,495 ft.—more than 3 times the height of New York's Empire State Building.

Would you dare to walk on this glass walkway, thousands of feet above the ground on the side of a cliff at Tianmen Mountain, China?

^ MESA VERDE, USA

CLIFFSIDE
HOMES

Mesa Verde in North America is famous for its ancient cliff dwellings, which are carved into caves and overhanging cliffs. People inhabited them around a thousand years ago.

^ MATERA, ITALY

10,000 YEARS OLD

The prehistoric cliffside cave homes of Matera, Italy, are still inhabited today. You can stay in a hotel there, sleeping where Stone Age people once slept.

LIFE ON THE
EDGE!

People love to live beside the sea—but cliffs erode! Houses with a sea view may one day find themselves hanging on the edge.

UNDERGROUND CAVES

Millions of caves are hidden beneath Earth's surface. Most are unexplored secrets, but here are some spectacular ones that have been found. New caves are being discovered all the time!

? *The Jenolan Caves are around 340 million years old, the oldest open caves ever discovered.*

JENOLAN CAVES

JENOLAN CAVES, AUSTRALIA

THE JENOLAN CAVES COVER 25 MILES, AND NEW SECTIONS ARE STILL BEING DISCOVERED

CAVE SYSTEMS ARE CREATED WHEN WATER GRADUALLY EATS AWAY SOFT LIMESTONE ROCK UNDERGROUND

FACT FILE

1. Water seeping through a cave picks up particles from the rock.

2. As the water evaporates, the particles build up on the ceiling. Icicle-like stalactites grow downward, and as they drip stalagmites grow upward from below. Sometimes they connect and form a column.

3. Stalactites grow around 1 in. every 100 years.

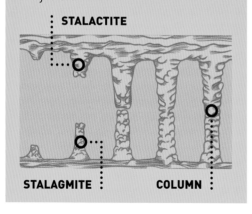

STALACTITE

STALAGMITE   COLUMN

CAVE ZONES

ENTRANCE ZONE

Cool and shaded, with some sunlight and plants. Temporary residents could include bats, frogs, beetles, and moths.

TWILIGHT ZONE

Damp, with low light. Worms and spiders may live here.

DARK ZONE

No light at all, and always the same chilly temperature. Can be home to tiny shrimps and blind fish.

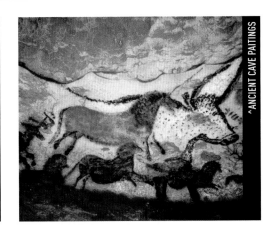

^ANCIENT CAVE PAINTINGS

983
FEET LONG

The size of crystal pillars found in the Naica Mine Caves in Mexico.

DEEPEST

Krubera Cave near the Black Sea is the deepest cave in the world. It has a recorded depth of 7,185 ft.

You could stack the Eiffel Tower in Paris, France, 6½ times on top of itself in the cave.

LONGEST
400 MILES

The Mammoth Cave system is the longest cave network in the world, deep beneath Kentucky, USA. It takes about a week to explore.

30,000 YEARS OLD

Caves containing ancient paintings by humans have been found on every continent except Antarctica. The paintings are usually of animals such as bulls, horses, and deer. Early humans hunted these creatures.

THE CAVES ARE FULL OF HUGE STALACTITES AND STALAGMITES

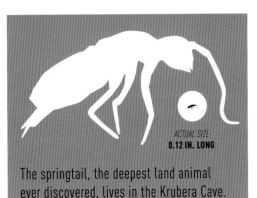

ACTUAL SIZE
0.12 IN. LONG

The springtail, the deepest land animal ever discovered, lives in the Krubera Cave.

1 MONTH

How long it takes for cavers to reach the bottom of Krubera. They describe it as like climbing an upside-down Everest.

🌍 FROZEN NORTH

It's always chilly in the Arctic Circle, the far north of the world, because there's never any strong sunlight. During the winter months it stays dark there day and night, and the Arctic Sea freezes over.

THE ARCTIC

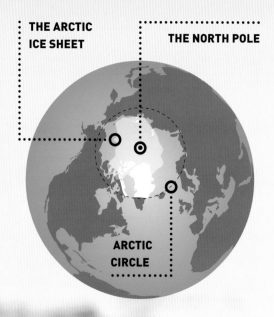

THE ARCTIC ICE SHEET

THE NORTH POLE

ARCTIC CIRCLE

YOU'LL ONLY FIND POLAR BEARS IN THE FAR NORTH OF THE WORLD, NEVER THE FAR SOUTH

🤖 FACT FILE

▲ The Arctic Circle marks the latitude north of which the sun does not rise in midwinter.

▲ Parts of the Arctic Ocean are always frozen, but large areas only freeze over in winter.

▲ **6 MILLION SQ. MILES**
Approximate extent of winter Arctic ice.

▲ **2.3 MILLION SQ. MILES**
Approximate extent of summer Arctic ice.

 PENGUINS ONLY LIVE IN THE SOUTHERN HEMISPHERE, SO PENGUINS AND POLAR BEARS ONLY EVER MEET UP IN ZOOS

 The word "Arctic" comes from the Greek word arktos, *meaning bear, but isn't named after polar bears. It is actually named after two star constellations, the Great Bear and Little Bear, seen in the Arctic sky.*

Icebergs break off the pack ice when the sun starts to melt it in the summer months.

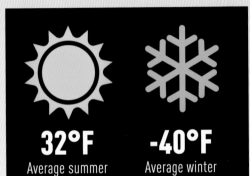

32°F
Average summer temperature

-40°F
Average winter temperature

430 MILES

>>>>>>>>>>>>>

The distance between the North Pole, the northernmost point on Earth, and the nearest land, Kaffeklubben Island (Greenland). The North Pole is located on permanently frozen ice.

THE ARCTIC 8

There are eight countries bordering the Arctic Circle—the USA (Alaska), Canada, Greenland, Iceland, Norway, Finland, Sweden, and Russia.

^ ARCTIC FOX

Some creatures, such as Arctic foxes and musk oxen, tough out the bad weather and stay in the Arctic through the winter. Others, such as reindeer, migrate south.

TYPES OF **ICE**

When the sea freezes over, different types of ice form.

FRAZIL ICE
Fine ice crystals suspended in sea water.

GREASE ICE
A thin, soupy layer of ice crystals which covers the water the way an oil slick does.

PANCAKE ICE
Circles of ice which are formed when grease ice is compressed by wind and waves.

PACK ICE
When pancake ice circles merge and freeze to form a solid floating surface.

SHIVERY SLUMBER

Would you like to sleep on an ice bed? Well, that's what you get if you visit an ice hotel in the Arctic. The buildings are built of snow and ice and are rebuilt each year.

^ ARCTIC HOTEL

^ PANCAKE ICE

ICE *SURFING*

Check out iceberg wakeboarding on the internet! You'll find crazy wakeboarders riding over and under icebergs.

ICEBOUND SOUTH

Antarctica is the continent in the far south of the world. There are so many glaciers there that they've merged into enormous seas of ice, called ice sheets.

ANTARCTICA

 FACT FILE

AVERAGE CLIMATE

▲ **ICE DEPTH**: 1 mile

▲ **WIND SPEED**: 50 mph

▲ **ANNUAL TEMPERATURE**: -56°F

? *Antarctica doesn't have a permanent population, but about 4,000 people inhabit research stations over the summer. Fewer than 1,000 stay in wintertime.*

? *Since it never rains in Antarctica, the region is actually a desert.*

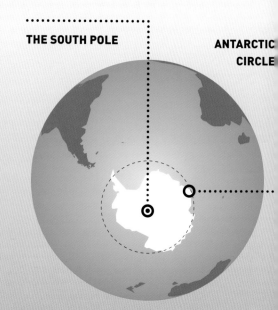

THE SOUTH POLE

ANTARCTIC CIRCLE

TOWERING ICEBERGS, MANY THE SIZE OF HOUSES, RISE UP OUT OF THE OCEAN

ICEBERGS ARE CONSTANTLY MOVING, BLOWN BY WIND OR CARRIED BY WATER CURRENTS

MOST OF AN ICEBERG'S ICE IS HIDDEN UNDER THE SEA

ICEBREAKERS

During Antarctic winters, powerful ice-breaking ships force a pathway through the sea ice to bring supplies to the frozen continent.

-128.6°F

The lowest temperature ever recorded on Earth, at Vostok Station, Antarctica.

200 MPH

The top wind speed in Antarctica, the windiest place on the planet.

5.4 MILLION
sq. miles

The area of the Antarctic ice sheet, about the size of the USA and Mexico combined.

90%

The amount of Earth's ice that covers Antarctica.

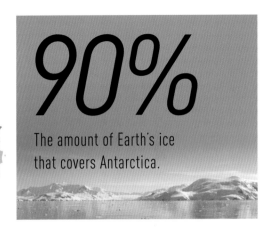

525
FEET WIDE

The crater width of Mount Erebus, Earth's southernmost volcano, on Antarctica. A lake of molten lava bubbles in the crater, which is 328 ft. deep.

^ GENTOO PENGUIN

22 mph

The speed at which Gentoo penguins can swim underwater. They hold the record for the fastest penguin swimmers.

FROZEN

Tiny vertebrates such as mites and ticks survive the winter by staying frozen under rocks and stones until the ice begins to melt. Antifreeze in their bodies prevents them from freezing to death.

Antarctica is the home of penguins. They are only found in the southern hemisphere.

🌐 ICE RIVERS

A glacier is a large, powerful river of ice, but it flows so slowly you can't see it move.

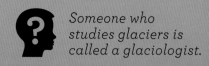 Someone who studies glaciers is called a glaciologist.

 **FACT FILE**

GLACIER TYPES

◢ **ALPINE GLACIERS**
run along mountain valleys.

◢ **ICE CAPS** (or ice fields)
are less than 20,000 sq. miles in size and sit on top of mountains.

◢ **ICE SHEETS** (or continental glaciers)
are usually found at the poles and are larger than 20,000 sq. miles.

PERITO MORENO GLACIER

A GLACIER CARVES A WIDE VALLEY INTO THE LANDSCAPE IT PASSES THROUGH, GATHERING UP PEBBLES AND ROCKS ALONG THE WAY

PERITO MORENO GLACIER, ARGENTINA

99% ❄️ 💧
The percentage of the planet's glacial ice located in the world's polar regions.

75% Amount of Earth's freshwater supply stored in glaciers.

In 2013, a 39,000-year-old woolly mammoth was discovered in Siberian glacial ice. Even its fur was preserved.

CALVING

‹‹‹‹‹‹‹‹‹‹‹

When a large chunk of ice breaks away from a glacier and becomes an iceberg.

HIDDEN **DANGER!**

Glacial cracks, or crevasses, can reach more than 98 ft. deep. These gaping ice holes are a hazard because they're often covered over by snow bridges that look safe to cross.

THE PERITO MORENO GLACIER IS 19 MILES LONG AND IS A TOP TOURIST ATTRACTION IN ARGENTINA

WORLDWIDE *COOL*

Glaciers are found on every continent of the world, even Africa. There's a small glacier near the summit of Mount Kilimanjaro, in Africa.

DEEP INSIDE A GLACIER THERE MAY BE ICE CAVES

 About 10% of Earth's surface is covered with glaciers.

^ GLACIER ICE CAVE, ALASKA

People can get married inside a glacier ice cave in Langjokull, Iceland, Europe's second largest glacier. The cave is man-made, and visitors are taken inside by a monster truck.

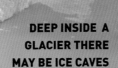

AVALANCHE!

When snow suddenly begins to race downhill at high speed it is called an avalanche or snowslide. The powerful snow flow can be deadly to anyone caught in its path.

Noises rarely cause avalanches, but cracking sounds could mean there's a snowslide on its way soon.

SNOW AVALANCHE

CAUCASUS MOUNTAINS, RUSSIA

FACT FILE

WHAT CAUSES SNOW AVALANCHES?

◣ **HEAVY SNOWFALL**—90% of snowslides occur during snowstorms.

◣ **STEEP SLOPES**—increase the speed of snow sliding downward.

◣ **SNOW LAYERING**—when fresh snow lands on top of ice and soon begins sliding.

◣ **VIBRATIONS**—these could be caused by people, such as skiers, disturbing the snow.

◣ **WIND**—Wind can deposit lots of snow in one place until it becomes so heavy it starts to slide.

AN AVALANCHE USUALLY BEGINS WHEN MELTED SNOW BREAKS AWAY IN LARGE SLABS FROM THE GROUND BELOW

AVALANCHES, SUCH AS THIS ONE IN THE CAUCASUS MOUNTAINS, POSE GREAT DANGER

AS THE SNOW FLOWS DOWN THE MOUNTAIN IT SPEEDS UP

80 mph ▶▶▶▶

The speed a sliding snow mass can reach in just 5 seconds. A big avalanche coming toward you is said to sound like an oncoming freight train!

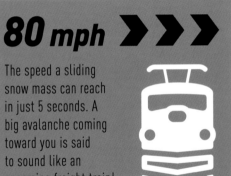

10,000

avalanches occur every year in the Swiss Alps.

LARGE CRACKS, OR FISSURES, APPEAR IN THE SNOW AS IT STARTS TO MOVE

1970

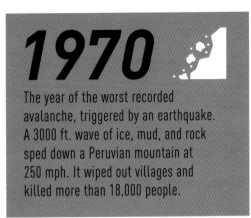

The year of the worst recorded avalanche, triggered by an earthquake. A 3000 ft. wave of ice, mud, and rock sped down a Peruvian mountain at 250 mph. It wiped out villages and killed more than 18,000 people.

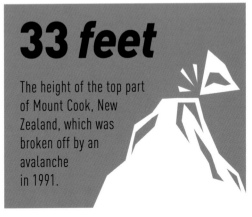

Scientists study the snow for signs of avalanche risk so they can warn people to stay away.

Snow fences are erected along danger zones to break up snowslides and redirect them away from villages.

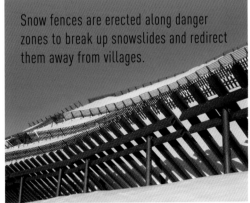

33 feet

The height of the top part of Mount Cook, New Zealand, which was broken off by an avalanche in 1991.

BY THE TIME SNOW REACHES THE BOTTOM OF THE MOUNTAIN, IT IS FINE AND POWDER-LIKE

RESCUE

▶▶▶▶▶▶▶▶▶▶▶

People can quickly become buried in an avalanche, so they need to be found as fast as possible. Rescue dogs are trained to sniff out trapped victims.

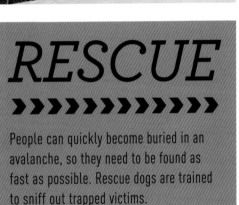

🌍 SAND WORLD

Huge, wind-swept, rippling sand mounds are common in deserts and coastal landscapes. Sand dunes can be as tall as mountains and bigger than some countries.

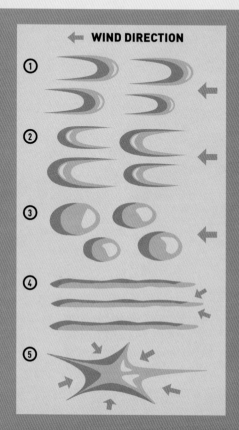

SAND DUNES

GOBI DESERT, MONGOLIA

DROUGHT-RESISTANT PLANTS CAN LIVE ON SAND DUNES, AND SOME SPECIES STORE RAINWATER IN THEIR LEAVES AND STEMS

🤖 FACT FILE

1. Sand dunes form in areas where there are large amounts of loose sand (most common along coastlines or in dried-up rivers, lakes, or sea beds).

2. Wind lifts and carries the sand grains, blowing it into heaps.

3. A sandy hill grows and forms a barrier against the wind.

4. Eventually the top of the mound collapses and slides down the sheltered side of the slope, known as the slip face.

5. A strong wind can change the shape of a sand dune overnight.

SAND DUNE TYPES

1. CRESCENT OR BARCHAN DUNE—
The most common type, shaped like a crescent moon, formed when winds blow from one direction.

2. PARABOLIC OR BLOWOUT DUNE—
U-shaped with an upward-pointing crest and elongated arms trailing behind it, usually with some plants.

3. DOME DUNE—rare, oval- or circular-shaped. Usually only a few feet high.

4. LINEAR OR SEIF DUNE—long, snakelike ridges, some 100 miles long.

5. STAR DUNE—star-shaped with a central peak, formed by winds blowing in different directions. Among the tallest dunes in the world.

← **WIND DIRECTION**

① ② ③ ④ ⑤

Sandstorms are common in hot, dry regions, such as the Sahara Desert. Strong winds whip up the top layer of sand or soil and can carry choking clouds of the dust for many miles.

5 MILLION YEARS OLD

The age of the sand at Big Daddy sand dune in the world's oldest desert, the Namib Desert in Namibia, Africa.

One of the toughest foot races in the world is the Marathon des Sables, run partly over sand dunes in the Sahara. It lasts six days and covers 156 miles.

SAND DUNES REACH UP TO 2620 FT. HIGH IN THE SOUTH GOBI DESERT, MONGOLIA

In 1994, competitor Mauro Prospero got lost in a sandstorm while running the Marathon des Sables. He survived for days by drinking urine and bat's blood.

THE GOBI SAND DUNES ARE WELL KNOWN FOR THEIR WHISTLING, SINGING, AND BOOMING—THE NOISES ARE CAUSED BY THE TOP LAYER OF SAND SLIDING OVER THE ONE BELOW, USUALLY IN STRONG WINDS

TOP 7 **TALLEST** SAND DUNES

1. CERRO BLANCO, Peru.................................... **3,860 ft.**

2. CERRO MEDANOSO, Atacama Desert, Chile .... **1,805 ft.**

3. BADAIN JARAN, China .... **1,640 ft.**

4. RIG-E YALAN DUNE, Iran...................................... **1,542 ft.**

5. ISAOUANE-N-TIFERNINE SAND SEA, Algeria .... **1,526 ft.**

6. BIG DADDY, NAMIBIA, Africa.................................... **1,066 ft.**

7. MOUNT TEMPEST, Australia .... **920 ft.**

SAND *WAVES*

Underwater dunes called sand waves are found under the Golden Gate Bridge, San Francisco, USA. There are 40 giant dunes up to 33 ft. high, and they are among the largest underwater sand waves found so far.

🌍 SALT WORLD

Large dried-out salt lakes, called salt flats or salt pans, are found in desert regions around the world. They are formed when water evaporates, leaving salt behind.

The area was once a giant prehistoric lake that has evaporated, leaving the salt behind.

SALAR DE UYUNI SALT PAN

BOLIVIA'S VAST SALAR DE UYUNI SALT PAN IS THE LARGEST ON THE PLANET

THE LANDSCAPE IS A VAST EXPANSE OF FLAT, GLISTENING SALT, HERE GATHERED INTO PILES FOR USE

SALAR DE UYUNI, BOLIVIA

OCCASIONALLY A THIN FILM OF RAINWATER COVERS THE SALT, AND SALAR DE UYUNI BECOMES THE WORLD'S BIGGEST MIRROR, REFLECTING THE SKY PERFECTLY

🤖 FACT FILE

◢ **4,086 SQ. MILES**
The area covered by Salar de Uyuni.

◢ **10 BILLION TONS**
The amount of salt at Salar de Uyuni.

◢ **50% TO 70%**
The percentage of the world's supply of the mineral lithium found underneath the salt at Salar de Uyuni. Mobile phones and computers contain lithium.

SALT HOTEL

Tourists can stay in a salt hotel on Salar de Uyuni. They can sleep on salt beds and sit on salty chairs!

Salar de Uyuni is home to vast flocks of pink flamingos.

Salt has been excavated at the Danakil Depression, Ethiopia, for centuries. At one time salt bars were the country's main form of currency.

DANGER!

The crusty top layer of a salt pan may disguise a muddy bog below.

^ STREAMLINER BIKE DESIGNED FOR AN ATTEMPT AT A LAND SPEED RECORD AT BONNEVILLE.

THE DEVIL'S GOLF COURSE

America's largest salt flat sits on the floor of Death Valley in California. The surface is covered in jagged rock-salt formations, and the salt pan was named after a quote that "only the devil could play golf" on it.

376.4 mph

The world motorcycle land speed record, set by Rocky Robinson on Bonneville Salt Flats in Utah, USA. The salt flats are regularly used for motorbike, truck, and car land speed record attempts.

^ DEVILS GOLF COURSE, DEATH VALLEY, CALIFORNIA.

🌍 WORLD'S WEIRDEST LANDSCAPES

With all the bizarre and wonderful structures that make up our planet, there's always something new and exciting to discover! Here are some unique places to put on your "must visit" list.

MOUNT RORAIMA PLATEAU

MOUNT RORAIMA, VENEZUELA

MOUNT RORAIMA IS A UNIQUE GIANT PLATEAU, RISING 1,200 FT. ABOVE THE FOREST FLOOR

SHEER CLIFFS RISE ON ALL FOUR SIDES OF THE PLATEAU

IT RAINS ALMOST EVERY DAY ON THE SURFACE OF RORAIMA—HOME TO ANGEL FALLS, THE WORLD'S HIGHEST WATERFALL (SEE PG. 11)

 FACT FILE

▲ Mount Roraima plateau rocks are 2 billion years old, one of the oldest geological formations in the world.

▲ The plateau stretches for 12 sq. miles.

They call the plateau the "Lost World." It has inspired novels and movies, because there are unique animals and plants that live there and nowhere else on Earth.

Tales from European explorers inspired Arthur Conan Doyle to write *The Lost World* in 1912. He imagined a hidden plateau where prehistoric dinosaurs roamed!

^ TIANZI MOUNTAINS, CHINA

24 MILLION YEARS

The age of the colorful, candy-striped Danxia Landform in China (below). The vibrant rock layers are caused by red sandstone and mineral deposits.

^ ZHANGYE DANXIA NATIONAL PARK, CHINA

4,140 FEET HIGH

The tallest peak of the towering pillar-shaped Tianzi Mountains of China. The incredible stone towers have been eroded by water over many centuries.

^ GIANT'S CAUSEWAY, IRELAND

LOST CITY

Deep in the Cambodian jungle lie the remains of the ancient city of Angkor. Abandoned in the 1400s, the stunning temples and statues have long since been swallowed up by jungle strangler figs.

40,000+

The number of hexagonal boulders in Giant's Causeway, Ireland. Legend tells of how giant Fin MacCoul made the stepping stones so he could walk across the sea to his enemy in Scotland. The rocks were actually formed by an ancient volcanic eruption.

^ LOST CITY OF ANGKOR, CAMBODIA

🌍 SHAPED BY NATURE

When land is eroded—worn down by wind, water, or ice—
weird and wonderful landscapes are sometimes created.

 *Strangely-shaped pillars
of rock, formed by erosion,
are called hoodoos.*

🤖 FACT FILE

TYPES OF EROSION

◢ COASTAL EROSION
Waves wear away the coastline.

◢ WIND EROSION
Wind erosion is common in deserts,
where sand is blown about.

◢ GLACIAL EROSION
Glaciers carve out the ground
beneath them (see pg. 46). They
create flat-bottomed valleys.

ARCHES NATIONAL PARK

< DOUBLE ARCH, ARCHES NATIONAL PARK

**ARCHES NATIONAL PARK,
UTAH, USA**

**"THE LANDSCAPE ARCH" IS
290 FT. WIDE, THE LONGEST
ARCH IN THE PARK**

**THE ARCHES HAVE
BEEN WORN INTO
SHAPE OVER TIME
BY RAIN**

**ARCHES NATIONAL PARK HAS
OVER 2,000 NATURAL SANDSTONE
ARCHES, THE GREATEST NUMBER
IN THE WORLD**

The "Fairy Chimneys" in Cappadocia, Turkey, are rock pillars sculpted by wind and rain. You can stay in a "Fairy Chimney" hotel.

^ BRYCE CANYON, USA

11x The jagged rock pillars, or hoodoos, in Bryce Canyon, USA, reach up to 200 ft. high. That's around 11 times taller than an adult male giraffe!

Inviting turquoise pools perch on top of white cliffs at Pamukkale in Turkey. The cliffs were formed by hot spring waters leaving behind calcium deposits. People have bathed in the warm pools for thousands of years.

^ PAMUKKALE, TURKEY

BENDING **BEACH**

Tidal currents and wind constantly reshape the Golden Horn sandbar at Zlatni Rat Beach, Croatia. The tip of the sandbar usually points eastward but sometimes, in strong winds, it turns to the west.

^ MONO LAKE, CALIFORNIA

SAND TUFA

These unique wind-sculpted towers (left) rise out of Mono Lake in California. They're made of calcium carbonate deposited by an underground freshwater spring before the lake's water level receded.

^ GOLDEN HORN SANDBAR, CROATIA

The Moeraki Boulders litter Koehohe Beach in New Zealand, weighing up to 7 tons. In Maori legend, they are said to be eel baskets washed ashore from a giant sailing canoe. They were actually formed on the seabed and erosion has left them on the beach.

🌐 UNSOLVED MYSTERIES

There's not much of our planet that we haven't explored, and scientists have explained many mysteries that puzzled our ancestors. However, there are still some places that baffle our brains!

THE CHOCOLATE HILLS

 One legend says that the hills were created by two giants who threw sand and stones at each other and left their mess behind them. Another claims the hills are a giant's teardrops.

THE CHOCOLATE HILLS, BOHOL, PHILIPPINES

THERE ARE BETWEEN 1,268 AND 1,776 OF THESE MYSTERIOUS GRASS-COVERED, CONE-SHAPED HILLS THAT NOBODY CAN EXPLAIN

THE MOUNDS ARE 98–164 FT. HIGH, WITH THE TALLEST REACHING 390 FT

THE GRASS-COVERED HILLS TURN BROWN IN THE DRY SEASON, HENCE THE NAME "CHOCOLATE"

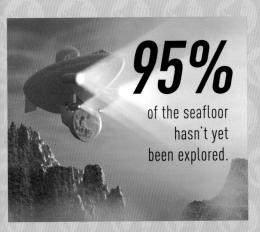

95%
of the seafloor hasn't yet been explored.

DEEP SEA *LAKE*

Daikoku volcano lies 1,358 ft. down in the Mariana Trench (see pg. 19). It's the only place on our planet that contains a molten sulfur lake. Scientists are unable to investigate it fully due to bubbling temperatures of 369°F.

^ ANTARCTICA

Follow the light

A mysterious, football-sized glowing sphere of light, the Min Min light, sometimes follows travelers through the Outback in Queensland, Australia. No one is sure where it comes from, but legend says that if you chase the Min Min light and catch it, you'll disappear!

^ DEATH VALLEY, USA

SECRET **LAKE**

Two miles beneath the Antarctic lies a secret world of lakes and rivers. Scientists have been trying to sample the lake water, trapped a million years ago by climate change, to perhaps find unknown bacteria.

MYSTERY **SOLVED!**

It took 70 years to crack the mystery of the sailing stones in Death Valley, USA. No one understood how the stones shuffled across the lakebed on their own, until scientists realized that a specific combination of water, ice, and wind was needed.

LOST KINGDOM

Papua New Guinea is home to a huge diversity of wildlife—some even claim to have spotted flying dinosaurs! In 2009, scientists found a 2-mile-wide crater teeming with 40 new plant and animal species, including a fanged frog.

^ AMAZON RAINFOREST

UNTOUCHED WORLD

Huge areas of the South American Amazon rainforest remain unexplored. It's thought there are likely to be many undiscovered animal species living there. We know from aerial surveys that there are tribes living in the jungle who have never had contact with the outside world.

GLOSSARY

AFTERSHOCKS The small earth tremors that occur after a larger earthquake.

ANTARCTICA The southernmost part of Earth, and the site of the South Pole.

ARCTIC CIRCLE The northernmost part of the planet, and the site of the North Pole.

AVALANCHE Snow that suddenly races downhill at great speed.

BLOWHOLE Small hole, commonly at the end of a sea cave, that ejects a fountain of water when pressure builds up below it.

BLUE HOLE An underwater sinkhole (a giant hole with steep vertical sides).

BOG Soft, wet, muddy ground.

BOX CANYON A small canyon with steep cliff walls on at least three sides.

CALVING When a large chunk of ice breaks away from a glacier and becomes an iceberg.

CANYON A deep and narrow, steep-sided valley carved out of rock by a river.

CARAT A unit of weight, equal to 0.007 oz., used to measure gemstones and gold.

CAVE A hollow opening or passage into the earth or under the ground.

CENOTE A water-filled sinkhole connected to underground caves and streams.

CHALLENGER DEEP The deepest point on Earth's seabed. It's located at the bottom of the Mariana Trench in the Pacific Ocean.

CLIMATE CHANGE A rise in the world's temperatures, probably caused by an increase in certain gases in our atmosphere.

CRUST Earth's outer layer, which is made up of rock.

EARTHQUAKE A sudden release of energy from Earth's crust that causes tremors and vibrations.

EPICENTER A point on Earth's surface where pressure is released during an earthquake.

EROSION When land is worn down by rain, wind, waves, or ice.

FISSURE A long, narrow crack or opening.

FOCUS A place inside the Earth's crust where pressure is released, often leading to an earthquake.

GEYSER A fountain of hot water that shoots up in the air from an underground spring.

GLACIER A large, slow-moving river of ice.

GLACIOLOGIST Someone who studies glaciers.

GORGE A narrow, steep-sided valley.

HOODOO A pillar of rock formed by erosion.

HOT SPRING Warm water that bubbles up from below the ground.

HURRICANE A large, powerful storm with extremely strong winds.

ICEBERG A large, floating mass of ice that has broken away from a glacier or sheet of ice.

ICE CAP A huge mass of snow and ice that permanently covers a large region of land.

ICE SHEET A large, thick mass of ice that covers a region.

KARST Cave widened by water erosion.

MAELSTROM A powerful whirlpool.

MAGMA Boiling liquid rock.

MANTLE Thick layer of liquid rock that lies below Earth's crust.

MARIANA TRENCH The deepest part of Earth, situated in the western Pacific Ocean.

MARSH Soft, wet, grassy land.

MOONBOW A rainbow that appears at night.

MOUTH The point where a river flows into a lake, reservoir, sea, or another river.

PACK ICE A large mass of ice floating on the sea, made up of smaller chunks of ice that have frozen together.

PEAT Partly decomposed vegetable matter, usually mosses, found in bogs. Peat is sometimes burned as fuel or mixed into soil to improve growing conditions.

PINNACLE A tall, pointed rock formation formed by erosion.

PLATEAU Flat-topped mountain peak.

PUMICE Air-filled volcanic stone that is so light it can float.

QUICKSAND Loose, wet sand that's unable to support weight, so anything landing on it gets sucked in.

RICHTER SCALE A method used to measure the strength of an earthquake.

RING OF FIRE An area of the Pacific Ocean encircled with volcanoes.

ROCK SPIRE A rock formation shaped like a spire, formed by erosion.

SALT FLATS (OR PANS) A large, flat area of land covered in salt, which has been left when water evaporated.

SANDBAR A ridge of sand in a river or ocean caused by waves and currents.

SAND DUNE A mound of sand that has been swept up by winds.

SINKHOLE The opening left behind when earth suddenly disappears below ground.

SLOT CANYON A narrow corridor formed by bursts of rushing water.

SNOWSLIDE An avalanche of snow.

SOURCE The start of a stream or river, usually high up in the mountains.

STALACTITE An icicle-shaped mineral deposit that hangs down from the roof of a cave.

STALAGMITE A mineral deposit that sits on the bottom of a cave and grows upward.

STORM SURGE An abnormal rise in coastal sea levels caused by a severe storm.

STRAIT A narrow channel of water connecting two seas.

SUBMARINE CANYON A canyon found on the seafloor.

SUBMERSIBLE An underwater vessel, used for exploring and working in deep seas.

SWAMP Saturated (very wet) land that is usually overgrown with vegetation.

TECTONIC PLATES Large, slow-moving plates that make up Earth's surface.

TSUNAMI A giant wave caused by an earthquake or major landslip.

VOLCANO A mountain that may sometimes shoot out hot rocks, ash, and lava from underneath the Earth's crust.

WATERFALL When river or stream water gushes down a steep drop.

WETLAND A low-lying area of wet land such as a swamp, bog, or marshland.

WHIRLPOOL Spinning water caused by currents.

INDEX

ACKNOWLEDGMENTS

PICTURE CREDITS:

KEY – tl top left, tc top center, tr top right, cl center left, c center, cr center right, bl bottom left, bc bottom center, br bottom right.,

© **Shutterstock:** 4tl Subbotina Anna, 4tr Anna Morgan, 4c EpicStockMedia, 4cl Rainer Albiez, 4cr Denis Burdin, 4b tusharkoley, 5tr (robot icon) Eka panova, 6l Daniel J. Rao, 7l Thor Jorgen Udvang, 7b wong yu liang, 8c Dobroslawa Szulc, 8l PRILL, 8r Sergey Uryadnikov, 9l Dr. Morley Read, 9r Igor Jandric, 9b Gilles Paire, 10c Ronald Sumners, 11t Vadim Petrakov, 11c Vadim Petrakov, 12c Andresr, 13l szefei, 13r Scott Prokop, 14c johnbraid, 15t vicspacewalker, 15l Pichugin Dmitry, 15r Zastolskiy Victor, 15b Photovolcanica.com, 16c Zacarias Pereira da Mata, 17tl Dr_Flash, 17tr Aditya Singh, 17c karamysh, 17cr EpicStockMedia, 17b Linda Bucklin, 20c KPG_Payless, 21bl Wolfgang Berroth, 22c Wollertz, 22cl nicolas.voisin44, 23t tagstiles.com - S.Gruene, 23tr paul prescott, 23c Steve Allen, 23bl Ivan_Sabo, 23br Eric Isselee, 24c Prometheus72 / fpolat69, 25t Cico, 25r NigelSpiers, 25br Sparkling Moments Photography, 26c Rainer Albiez, 26l fluidworkshop, 27l Designua, 27ct 123dartist, 27cb In Green, 27br Sergios, 28c f11photo, 29t Lorcel, 29l Filip Fuxa, 29r Sean Pavone, 29b Patricia Hofmeester, 30c zebra0209, 31tr Matej Hudovernik, 31r ILeysen, 32c Filipe Frazao, 32l Eduard Kyslynskyy, 33tr Nicola Keegan, 33c John Wollwerth, 33tl Bennyartist, 33bl cellistka, 33b pio3, 34c dibrova, 35t Wolfgang Zwanzger, 35c Subbotina Anna, 35r AridOcean, 36c Daniel Prudek, 37tl Elzbieta Sekowska, 37b Frontpage, 38c Zalka, 39t Nadezda Murmakova, 39c vichie81, 39r Sumikophoto, 39bl KN, 40c e X p o s e, 40l michlomop, 41tr AISA - Everett, 42c La Nau de Fotografia, 43tl meunierd, 43c Josef Pittner, 43r Jorg Hackemann, 43b Volt Collection, 44c 140914756, 45l VikOl, 45tr Cico, 45r Denis Burdin, 45c ChameleonsEye, 45br BMJ, 46c Joshua Raif, 47tl Bernhard Staehli, 47tr Incredible Arctic, 47b saraporn, 48c My Good Images, 49 tr prochasson frederic, 49c Peter Gudella, 49br Cylonphoto, 50c Daniel Prudek, 50tr Daniel Prudek, 51tl onairda, 51tr Maridav, 51b Dudarev Mikhail, 52c Chris Howey, 53tl Alberto Loyo, 53tr Matej Hudovernik, 53c John Blanton, 53br Gary C. Tognoni, 54c Harald Toepfer, 54b leonello calvetti, 55tl lzf, 55r SIHASAKPRACHUM, 55b Noradoa, 55br R.M. Nunes, 56b Guoqiang Xue, 56c tusharkoley, 57tl meunierd, 57t Anna Morgan, 57r Mikael Damkier, 57c Scott Prokop, 57bl Simone Simone, 57br Khoroshunova Olga, 58c Khoroshunova Olga, 59tl Esteban De Armas, 59tr mattymeis, 59c Mariusz S. Jurgielewicz, 59bl Ammit Jack, 59br Linda Bucklin

© **Science Photo Library:** p18c Alexis Rosenfield p25bl Gary Hincks   © **CORBIS:** 19br Li Ziheng/Xinhua Press   **Mark A. Garlick:** 29c   **All other vector art © Shutterstock and Dynamo Limited**